Dedication

I want to dedicate this book to my children of whom I am very proud. Cydney-Elise Kiara Koné, Cheik Isaiah-Stephan Koné & Raven-Alexis Noel Koné. 4EVER4KIDS

In Loving Memory of my Beloved father Alphonso Spells, my Dearest father-in-laws Boubacar Koné and Richard Walker, my Cherished Grandmother Ida Mae Weatherspoon, and my truly adored instructors Grandmaster Kijuana Vita and Yucca. I love you all

I would also like to thank all of those individuals who made this book possible mainly Cheik Koné, Shawn Charney and my biggest fan and supporter, my sister Kesiha Crews.

Angelina the Anteater always ate artichokes, apples and avocados after her acrobatics, archery and Australian football.

Brad the Bobcat back flipped over a belly dancer from Babylon before bouncing bread on the balance beam at the beach.

Cameron the Canary was catapulted over the cottage near the creek after capturing a caboose full of chipmunks, Chihuahua's and camels on their way to a Canadian carnival.

Demi the Dinosaur dodged a delicious Danish while dancing to drummers in Downtown Delaware.

Eva the Elephant and Ethan the Elk enjoyed educating their earlobes and exercising their elbows in Europe.

Farrah the Ferret featured her favorite food...filet of fish at the fair in Fresno.

Gabrielle the Great Dane gave grape juice, garlic bread and gifts to the gardener, the gate keeper and the garbage collector.

Hugh the Hawk held his breath at the Hawthorne horse race for hours hoping that his horses, Hans Solo and Haley's comet would be victorious.

Isabella the Iguana was intrigued by ice which incited the idea to isolate herself in an igloo in Iceland only to exit for ice cream and ice skating.

Jennifer the Jaguar was a Jack-of-all-Trades. She joined a jazz band and they drove her jeep to a jam session in Jamaica where she jumped over a Jack-o-Lantern near a Japanese garden.

Kelsey the Kangaroo wore khakis to the Kentucky Derby with his kooky kids who brought kettle corn, kabobs, Kool-Aid and Kit Kats from the kitchen to keep themselves entertained

Lindsey the Llama lost her lovely locket while doing the limbo with the lean lawyer. She later left in a limo laughing loudly like a lunatic when she learned she had just won the lottery.

Madeleine the Monkey was on a mission to make as many mud pies as she could for her mean master's masquerade ball.

Natalie the Nightingale nibbled on nachos after nailing her audition for Napoleon. She then napped til noon.

Orlando the Octopus ate an omelet with orange juice and played "Old La Night" on the organ before his appointment with his optometrist.

Paula the Penguin was pleasantly plump, peculiar and a perfectionist. While wearing her pretty pink pea coat she ate pickles in her pasta primavera then painted a near perfect picture of a Picasso.

QUAIL QUALITY

Quentin the Quail played with his quartet quickly without quarrel so he could throw a quadruple twist before the highly anticipated quake.

Ray the Rhinoceros was responsible for regulating rebellious rabbits from raiding the refrigerator.

Sean the Sloth sailed the seven seas with his sword in his hand, a scarf 'round his neck and a satchel on his side.

Taylor the Tiger was tempted to taste the tantalizing tortellini left on the table next to the tabasco sauce.

Uma the Unicorn usually rode her unicycle through the Underground Railroad until she had an unlucky and untimely accident which caused her to upgrade to an Uplander.

Vince the Viper forgot to vaccinate before he vacationed in Venice where he bought vanilla wafers from the vending machine.

Wanda the Walrus wept while watching War of the Worlds through her neighbor's window.

Xena the Xerus (African ground squirrel) played the xylophone with her brother Xavier after her x-ray.

Yasmine the Yorkie went to Yale University and sang yankee doodle every year for the Yacht Club.

Zach the Zebra had zero tolerance for his zany friend Zelda who did everything with zeal. Zelda zipped on her zoot suit while Zach zoomed in and zapped the overzealous zombie.

Reflection Questions

1. List 3 things you remember from the story.

2. Name 2 places mentioned in the ABC Adventures.

3. Which list of characters had an adventure in the story?

   a) cat, llama, tiger, squirrel
   b) cat, rat, squirrel, mouse
   c) kangaroo, monkey, llama, zebra

4. Which list of characters is in alphabetical order?

   a) zebra, anteater, tiger, dinosaur
   b) anteater, dinosaur, tiger, zebra
   c) tiger, zebra, dinosaur, anteater

Bonus: What is a Xerus?

   a) Viper   c) Sloth
   b) Hamster   d) African ground squirrel

Writing Prompts

1. Write your own adventure using one of your favorite characters from the story.

2. Write 3-5 sentences that explain what you think took place after your favorite ABC characters adventure.

Hidden Pictures

Nachos Octopus Penguin Quail Rabbit Sailboat Tiger
Unicorn Vending Machine Walrus Xylophone Yorkie Zombie

Arrow   Bread   Canary   Drum   Elephant   Fish   Grape Juice
Horse   Ice Cream   Jack-o-Lantern   Kangaroo   Llama   Monkey

WORD SEARCH

```
A P P L E D S T A B L E M U D X R A Y K
P A N A I G L O O H W E P T Q W I J P Y
K S E S R O H B R R L U C O T T A G E A
I T V Q A D R E G E A B E A C H I E R N
T A E U B A N M A Z Z U N L U C K Y A K
C W S A B N E L E P H A N T V T F G W E
H W B I I I A S K L A W Y E R T P L M E
E D T L T S S O V A N I L L A P G I F T
N J E E P H T H O R G A N R H U M M E R
```

Apple	Elephant	Jeep	Nap	Rabbit	Vanilla	Yak
Beach	Gift	Kitchen	Organ	Seven	Wept	Zero
Cottage	Horse	Lawyer	Pasta	Table	X-Ray	
Danish	Igloo	Mud	Quail	Unlucky	Yankee	

www.ingramcontent.com/pod-product-compliance
Lightning Source LLC
LaVergne TN
LVHW071029070426
835507LV00002B/78